Duddy

Mike

Moomy

Chase

Callie

Lexi

Shawn

IMAGE CREDITS: PAGE 7: © OKSANA KUZMINA, © FAMVELDMAN, © SVITLANA, © LOUIS-PHOTO, © TIERNEY, PAGE 10: © MOODBOARD, © GERASIMOV174, © ZOOMTEAM, PAGE 11: © LIGHTFIELD STUDIOS, © OLEKSANDR, © LEARCHITECTO, © 103TNN, PAGE 14: © PROVECTORS, PAGE 15: © NRKZ, PAGE 62: © YAI, PAGE 128: © MEDELWARDI

LIBRARY OF CONGRESS CONTROL NUMBER: 2023944486
ISBN 978-0-06-334940-7

TYPOGRAPHY BY ERICA DE CHAVEZ WONG & CHRISSY KURPESKI
24 25 26 27 28 PC/WOR 10 9 8 7 6 5 4 3 2 1
FIRST EDITION

Oreo

Ollie

Table of Contents

Class Photo!

Oh, the Places We've Been!

FGTEEV

FGTEEV PRESENTS Goozy

APE CHASE

I'M DOWN WITH THE PEW

LETTERS

A Letter from
CRINGEY PRINCIPAL

DEAR **TROUBLEMAKERS!**

FIRST OFF, I'M **LOOKING FINE** IN THESE
FANCY ROBES. IN ADDITION, SINCE I
JUST GOT MY HAIR DID, I AWARD MYSELF
TOP HONORS FOR BEING **SO FLY**. BUT
I GUESS YOU'D LIKE TO HEAR ABOUT THE
GRADUATING CLASS OF **MISCREANTS** AND
RULE BREAKERS. ANOTHER YEAR, ANOTHER
DETENTION, IF YOU ASK ME. THIS GRADUATING
CLASS HAS CERTAINLY SET THE RECORD FOR
THE MOST VIOLATIONS OF THE STUDENT
HANDBOOK. **DO I GIVE OUT AN AWARD
FOR THAT?!**

THIS IS ALL TO SAY, **GOOD RIDDANCE
TO THIS CLASS OF SENIOR CLOWNS**.

CRINGELY,

CRINGEY PRINCIPAL

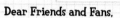

A Letter from Dean of Students,

FUNnel Boy

Dear Friends and Fans,

Forgive Cringey Principal! He meant to discuss the **wild ride** it's been for the **FGTeeV family**! From the **Nickelodeon Kids' Choice Awards** to the **YouTube Creator Awards**, from the **scariest video-game playthroughs** to the **catchiest songs**, the FGTeeV family has been on a roller coaster of fun.

In *FGTeeV: The Official Guidebook*, we'll take a trip through the family's **funniest moments, most iconic songs**, and **craziest adventures**—and even **learn some new things** about our favorite family. If you love to laugh and love to play, **join us!**

Cringey Principal and the rest of us would like to **thank the wonderful fans** for an incredible year, and congratulations to our wacky graduating class! **Funnel cakes for everyone!**

Yours truly,
Dean of Students

Skip McGiggleson (A.K.A. FUNnel Boy)

GRADUATING SENIORS

CONGRATS
ON A
WILD YEAR!

VINCENT

A.K.A. Duddy, Duddz,
FeeGee, Skylander Dad, FUNnel Dad

☠ IT'S OKAY TO MAKE MISTAKES, BUT HOW
YOU HANDLE THEM IS WHAT REALLY MATTERS! ☠

YUMS
- ✔ Gaming
- ✔ Editing
- ✔ Eating

YUCHS
- ✗ Dog poop in the yard
- ✗ When restaurants give small lemon slices in drinks (When life gives you lemons . . .)
- ✗ Too many dislikes to list them all! (I'm a perfectionist!)

FAVORITE GAME

ZANY FACTOIDS!

- I always have lint in my belly button! I'm a Swiss Army Knife of belly-button lint!
- When we go to a new restaurant, I *must* try *all* the appetizers.

SPECIAL TALENTS

- I kind of rhyme words together so I can say I'm a rapper
- Master organizer
- I can clear the room with a single fart (I'm One-Punch Man with my butt trumpet!)

SAMANTHA

A.K.A. Moomy, Not-So-Skylander
Mom, FUNnel Mom

*GOD GIVES HIS TOUGHEST BATTLES
TO HIS STRONGEST SOLDIERS.*

YUMS
- ✔ Tacos!
- ✔ Exercising!
- ✔ More Tacos!

YUCHS
- ✗ Folding laundry
- ✗ Squidy calamari (I'm talking about the tentacles! The round parts are okay. Haha!)
- ✗ Mom jeans
- ✗ Extremely slow drivers (I've got places to be!)
- ✗ When dishes are put next to the sink instead of *inside* the sink (I'm looking at you, DUDDY!!!)

FAVORITE GAME

All of them, because I'm the master of every single video game!  I *never* get stuck in random walls. I *always* know where I am. And I'm *super* skilled at pressing WASD. LOLZ!

ZANY FACTOID!

As a kid, frijoles con pata (beans with pigs' feet) was my favorite meal. Don't knock it until you've tried it! Yum!

SPECIAL TALENTS

- Singing
- Tacos! (That's a talent, right?)

⚡FEET?⚡

ALEXIS

A.K.A. Lexi, Lex, FGTeeV Lex,
Skylander Girl

★EVERYTHING HAPPENS FOR A REASON.★

YUMS

✔ Food!
✔ Hanging with friends
✔ Eating food with friends!
✔ Singing
✔ Singing with food!
✔ Traveling
✔ Music
✔ Taking pictures of food while traveling!
✔ Cooking food!
✔ Shopping
✔ I almost forgot, but I also like FOOD!

YUCHS

✗ Cucumbers (Not a food!)
✗ Reading (Unless it's something cool, like this book 📖)
✗ Haters
✗ Horror movies
✗ Slow walkers

FAVORITE GAME
Roblox *Prop Hunt X*

ZANY FACTOID!
I overcame my deathly fear of lobsters! And
you can too! (Not a lobster, but you get the idea!)

SPECIAL TALENTS
- Academics (Study hard, kids!)
- Singing
- Cooking
- Carrying this family with my humor

MICHAEL

A.K.A. Mike, Mickster

✗ THE WORD "CAN'T" IS <u>NOT</u> IN MY VOCABULARY. ✗

YUMS

✔ Boxing
✔ Football
✔ Candy!
✔ Collecting shoes
✔ Video games (duh!)
✔ Designing clothes
  & fashion

YUCHS

✗ Hates the fact that I
  don't hate anything . . .
  Wait a second . . .

FAVORITE GAME
Fortnite

TAPPA TAPPA TAPPA TAPPA TAPPA

GUM

BACK TO SCHOOL

DIY EDIBLE SUPPLIES

TunnelVision

ZANY FACTOID!
I once bought my classmates Valentine's Day candy but ended up eating it all myself when treats were banned that year.

SPECIAL TALENTS
- Singing
- Writing
- Upper cuts (Kapow!)

19

CHASE

A.K.A. LightCore Chase, FGTeeV Chase, Drizz McNizz, Drizzy, Chase–Tsu

 I'M SO <u>HUNGRY!</u>

YUMS

✔ Coding games on Scratch
✔ Playing *Roblox*
✔ Chilling with my cousins
✔ Basketball
✔ Fishing
✔ Pokémon cards
  (Gotta Catch 'Em All!)

YUCKS

✘ Eating fish
✘ Hiking

FAVORITE GAME
Roblox

ZANY FACTOID!
I can't fall asleep without the TV on.

SPECIAL TALENTS
Mathematics! I'm older now, but I still hold the title.

SHAWN

A.K.A. FGTeeV Shawn, Beasty,
Ghost Puncher

✳ I NEVER RISK IT FOR A BISCUIT! ✳

YUMS
✔ Soccer
✔ Christmas
✔ Pokémon
  cards (Gotta
  Catch 'Em All!)
✔ Hanging
  with cousins

YUCKS
✗ Going to
  bed before
  midnight!

FAVORITE GAMES
- *FIFA*
- *Fortnite*
- *Roblox*

Solo

Battle Royal

CONNECTING.

eases!

ZANY FACTOID!
Was born a little
bit yellow—like
a superhero!

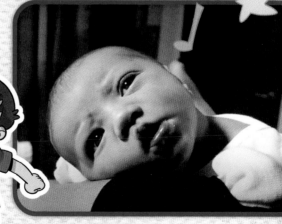

SPECIAL TALENTS
- Athletics
- Gaming

Awards & Honors

Valedictorians and salutatorians, record setters and undefeated champions, the **FGTeeV FAMILY** took the **HIGHEST HONORS** over the years. From the YouTube Creator Awards to the Roblox Bloxy Awards, our **STAR-STUDDED FAMILY** of titleholders took the cake and ate it too!

FUNnel CAKE CHALLENGE

JOIN US on a trip down the memory lane of champions as we return to the **FGTeeV FAMILY'S** greatest successes!

YOUTUBE SILVER PLAY BUTTON

YouTube Creator Awards, also known as **YouTube Play Buttons**, recognize the website's most popular channels. The **Silver Creator Award** goes to channels that reach or surpass one hundred thousand subscribers. **The FGTeeV family** has nine channels with one hundred thousand subscribers or more.

★ FGTeeV
★ FV Family
★ TheSkylanderBoy AndGirl
★ DOH MUCH FUN
★ FUNnel Boy & Friends
★ FUNnel Vision
★ Family Gaming SHORTS
★ Beasty Shawn
★ Toons + Tunes

YOUTUBE GOLD PLAY BUTTON

The **Gold Creator Award** (or **Gold Play Button**) goes to channels that reach or surpass a million subscribers. The **FGTeeV family** has five channels with one million subscribers or more.

★ FGTeeV
★ FV Family
★ TheSkylanderBoy AndGirl
★ DOH MUCH FUN
★ Family Gaming SHORTS

YOUTUBE DIAMOND PLAY BUTTON

The coveted **Diamond Creator Award** (or **Diamond Play Button**) goes to channels that reach or surpass ten million subscribers. The **FGTeeV channel** was the family's first channel to reach ten million subscribers!

10,000,005 FGTeeV

Here they are celebrating that milestone. Now FGTeeV is at twenty million subscribers and still growing!

The FV Family channel was the most recent FGTeeV channel to reach ten million subscribers!

Time to celebrate the glorious milestone! Where to? Shake Shack, of course!

SKYLANDERS KAOS TROPHY FOR ONE BILLION VIEWS

Skylanders is an action–adventure video game published by Activision, and the **FGTeeV family** loves battling through Skylands.

Activision gave us a custom Skylanders Kaos Trophy for surpassing a billion views!

THE ROBLOX BLOXY AWARD!

Roblox is an online game platform and game creation software that lets gamers program and play games created by other users. The **Bloxy Awards** is a yearly event held by Roblox to honor the artistic, creative, and social abilities of its gamers. The Roblox community votes for each award category, and the results are streamed on YouTube.

The FGTeeV family was nominated for the Roblox Video of the Year award for their banger "Psycho Pig."

SHE GOT THE CREEPIEST EYE

BLOXY WINNER
ROBLOX VIDEO OF THE YEAR

I'MMA FIND A NICE LITTLE SPOT ON THE COUCH AND SIT

FGTEEV
PSYCHO PIG

And guess who won the Bloxy!

THINK I WAS KIDNAPPED BY A PSYCHO PIG

You guessed it! "Psycho Pig"!

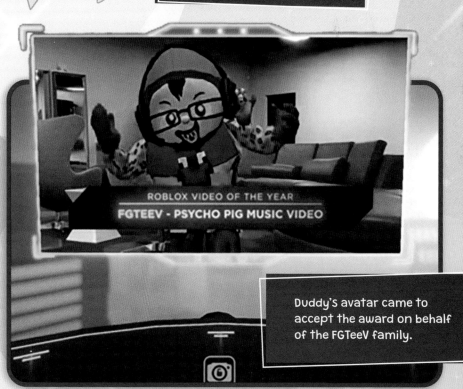

ROBLOX VIDEO OF THE YEAR
FGTEEV - PSYCHO PIG MUSIC VIDEO

Duddy's avatar came to accept the award on behalf of the FGTeeV family.

NICKELODEON KIDS' CHOICE AWARDS 2023

Nickelodeon is the first cable channel just for kids!
The **Nickelodeon Kids' Choice Awards** is a special event to give prizes to the year's biggest in television, film, music, and sports. Voted on by kids, the winners receive the **Nickelodeon Blimp**.

Guess who got nominated for the Favorite Social Media Family category? The FGTeeV family!

The award ceremony at Nickelodeon Studios was insane! I hope the FGTeeV family doesn't get slimed!

WE JUST GOT SLIMED

Oh well! That's what washing machines are for.

FGTEEV

FGTEEV

FGTEEV

FGTEEV

FGTEEV

FGTeeV on the big stage! Everyone is cheering for the world's favorite YouTube family. FGTeeV! FGTeeV! FGTeeV!

Wild on campus!

Some fans forget the most important members of the **FGTeeV FAMILY**: our four-legged furry friends! Our dogs **OREO, OLLIE,** and **CALLIE!**

Let's revisit some of our **FAVORITE MEMORIES** with the **BEST PUPS** in the YouTube biz.

OREO

Oreo is the OG canine of the FGTeeV clan and some say the cutest of the pack. She certainly thinks so.

She's always down to chill or get her face stuck in a cup!

If Oreo busts out of her prison cell, she'll come for you! Watch out!

HELLO LITTLE GOLDEN DOODLE

OLLIE

Ollie is the cutest goldendoodle you've ever seen and the biggest snuggle bunny of the bunch!

Look at that sweet face! Surely he's not up to anything . . . The attack is coming from inside the shirt!

Ollie is always down to give kisses, whether you like them or not. Thankfully, Duddy loves them!

CALLIE

Callie is the cutest little sister in the FGTeeV kennel.

She'd never instigate a fight with her beloved sibling Ollie. (She definitely would.) Round one: fight!

0.0%
Callie

When the FGTeeV family leaves the house, sometimes this sweet princess must go to puppy prison. Don't do the crime if you can't do the time.

student Life & clubs

BIRTHDAYS!

Nobody gets more hyped for birthdays than the FGTeeV crew! Duddy loves to celebrate with an extra-special b-day breakfast . . . and then things *always* go totally off the rails!

From indoor ball pits to submarine adventures, the **FGTeeV FAMILY** participates in more extracurricular activities than anyone in the world. **LET'S LOOK BACK** at the greatest **HIJINKS, HORSEPLAY,** and **SHENANIGANS** the **FGTeeV FAMILY** got up to!

SHOPPING CLUB!

Whether it's surprising strangers with a shopping spree or getting spooky in Spirit Halloween, the FGTeeV family knows just how to get their shop on! Shawn's a total natural: he's been building shopping skillz since his fingers were too small to use LEGO.

VACATION TEAM

When the FGTeeV family hits the road, it's go big or go home! From the shark—infested beach resorts to the nonstop thrill—ride adventures—if there were a trophy for #1 best vacationers ever, they would win it every time.

HIBACHI

HIBACHI & COOKING CLUB

Wherever they go, they're cooking up the awesome... The FGTeeV family are the HIBACHI KINGS! Chase even had a hibachi-themed backyard birthday party. Hibachi = heaven.

DRONE TEAM

It's a bird! It's a plane! Nope—it's a DRONE! Making a TOLIET PAPER FORT! Or maybe even getting EATEN BY ALLIGATORS! When the FGTeeV drone team hits the field, brace yourself for some wild hijinks.

ANIMATION STATION CLUB

The FGTeeV family are too cool to be contained to the real world . . . so they're also animated! Toons + Tunes is a totally rockin' channel full of music videos, animated stories from the real world, and creepy, crazy gaming moments.

45

HOLIDAYS

HELP!

When FUNnel Boy's ha-ha-has become ho-ho-hos, you know it's holiday time with the FGTeeV family. FUNnel Boy loves to get dressed up for the holidays . . . but not more than the FGTeeV family loves to go totally Hallo-wild on Halloween!

Oh yeah, FGTeeV family is gonna get their boogie on. Anytime, anyplace! Everyone knows how to bust a sick move, but their favorite has got to be Walk Like Shawn!

DANCE CLUB

SHAWN GOES GROCERY SHOPPING!

Duddy is out of hot sauce, so he takes his first mate, Shawn, to the grocery store to grab some more. What starts as a little trip to the market turns into a Shawn's first day of tomfoolery at the grocery store.

Hot sauce is all that Duddy needs, so surely that's all they'll get. Surely!

Shawn does need to resupply his candy. Gotta keep his hit points up!

"MY CANDY"

"YEAH, OREO!"

Shawn is making good choices at the grocery store! The FGTeeV family always needs more Oreos!

Shawn knows just how to make a balanced breakfast. Fruits and vegetables? Nah! More Mickey waffles!

"MICKEY WAFFLE!"

HE ALMOST HIT IT

Shawn almost crashes his cart but swerves just in time. It was almost a hit—and-run accident!

DIY EDIBLE SCHOOL SUPPLIES!

We've all been there. It's the first day of school, and you've got your candy supplies for the new year. But wait! Mr. Principal Joker takes the fun out of learning when he bans treats from class. That's okay—Duddy and Mike have cooked up some sweet ideas to sneak the confections back into school.

But Duddy and Mike are on the case! Together, they'll engineer a fail-safe plan to smuggle in their best treats.

Back to School
DIY EDIBLES

Mike

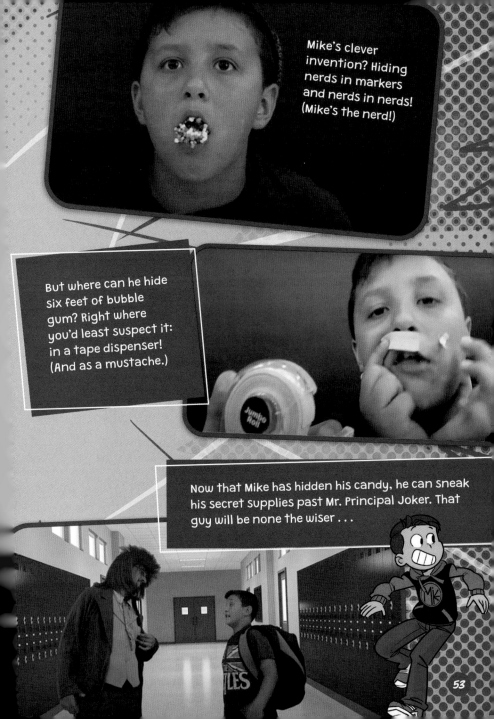

Mike's clever invention? Hiding nerds in markers and nerds in nerds! (Mike's the nerd!)

But where can he hide six feet of bubble gum? Right where you'd least suspect it: in a tape dispenser! (And as a mustache.)

Now that Mike has hidden his candy, he can sneak his secret supplies past Mr. Principal Joker. That guy will be none the wiser . . .

53

EATING ONLY ONE COLOR OF FOOD FOR 24 HOURS!!!

The FGTeeV family has thrown down the gauntlet! Each member of the family will draw a color and then for a full twenty-four hours they must eat only stuff in that color! If you like oranges, I sure hope you get the color orange. Game on!

Shawn draws the first color and gets white(ish)!

SHAWN'S COLOR: WHITE-ISH

PART ONE: SHOPPING

Duddy got pink, Mike got blue, Chase got brown (he was bummed until he remembered he can eat Nutella!), Moomy got orange, and then Shawn drew a few more colors for good measure. Now it's time to shop!

Shawn crashes into the counter with his WHITE marshmallows! Now that is a reckless driver! Or maybe I should say a wreckful driver!

Moomy wins lunch with her ORANGE cinnamon buns! It's hard to beat Moomy when she puts her mind to something.

MOMMY WINS LUNCH!

Duddy shares PINK ice cream with Oreo! The pup is color-blind, but she sure likes pink!

CHASE'S 6TH B-DAY

Chase, A.K.A. Drizzy, A.K.A. Chase–Tsu, is the second youngest of the FGTeeV clan. When he turned six, the family threw him a birthday party he would never forget.

Here's the birthday boy!

Chase got his very own Nintendo DS with a Mario case! Best birthday present ever! Time to pound those Goombas!

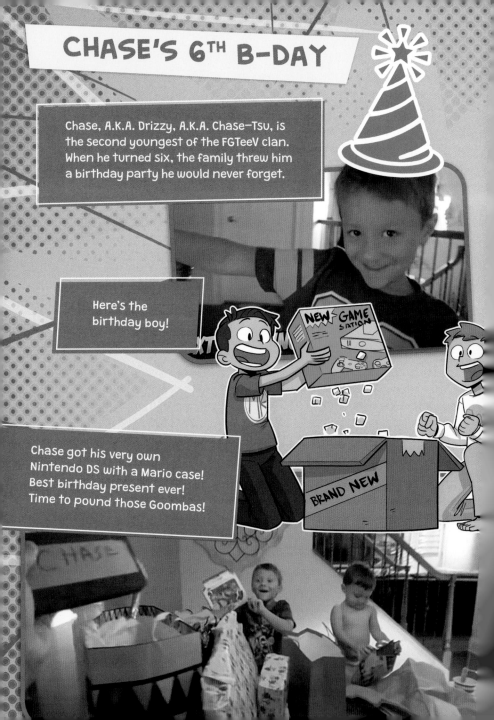

As is tradition in the FGTeeV family, Chase sprouted his vampire teeth on his sixth birthday. He's ready to suck the life out of . . . life!

For Chase, there's no better cake than an Oreo log.

Of course, the best way to end a perfect birthday is gaming with Duddy. Some quality father–son time!

DOWN WITH THE PEW

Shawn sure doesn't like bad guys. It's a good thing he's got ALL the Nerf Blasters to take 'em out. This little guy is down with the pew!

Officer Shawn is ready to take on the baddies. Locked and loaded!

Duddy and Shawn devise a plan to stand against anyone who causes trouble. Shoot their toys first and ask questions later.

IF YOU SEE A BAD GUY.

The bad guys broke into the house, but they won't stand a chance against Officer Shawn.

POW!

PEW, PEW, PEW!

SO HE'LL AIM TO STOP YA

You can't run from his Gatling gun! It might be overkill, but that's certainly better than underkill.

Even ghosts don't have a prayer against Officer Shawn. Back to your nether realm, you lost souls!

SHAWN BREAKS HIS CRIB

With a little bit of magic, Shawn breaks his crib. Just kidding! It's just time for Shawn to graduate to a big-boy bed.

First things first: Shawn goes to the furniture store to find the perfect bed frame to replace his crib.

Once Shawn finds the perfect bed, it's time to take apart his old crib . . . using Duddy magic!

Chase also gets an upgrade! He climbed the top of Mount Bedverest, where he can survey all the lands.

Shawn uses his dresser as a ladder to climb into his new bed! He too is a fearless mountaineer on the hills of Slumberland.

The kids found secret FGTeeV toys in their new nightstand. All their favorites are there!

SHARK SONG ON RAFT!

Raft is the name of the game, but shark is the name of the enemy. In this open world survival sandbox game, you must collect resources to buff up your raft while keeping away from any sharks ready to snack on you.

Duddy has drifted into the ocean and floats on his raft all alone. How does he spend his time? Singing a song on the open sea!

Duddy and Chase reporting for duty. The crew is ready to set sail on this video-game adventure.

TEASING ALLIGATORS WITH DRONE: BITE ME, PLEASE!

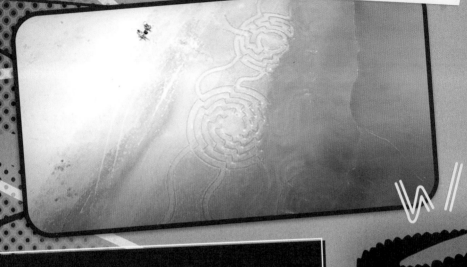

The FGTeeV family did something ah—MAZE—ing at the beach! You get it? It's a giant sand maze!

Duddy is bribing Chase and Shawn to finish their juice. They need their antioxidants—the archenemies of oxidants!

Duddy loves signing random FGTeeV books in the store. He hopes his pen doesn't run out of ink!

The family is being stalked by a gator! Time to turn tail and run!

The FGTeeV family escaped. But the alligator still might nibble on the family's drone.

ULTIMATE HIDE-AND-SEEK HACK + DEMOGORGON IN THE BACKYARD!

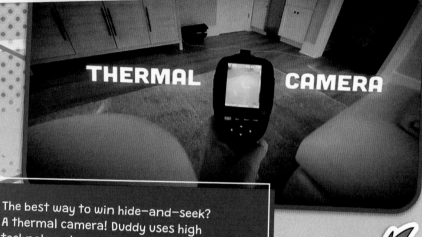

THERMAL CAMERA

The best way to win hide-and-seek? A thermal camera! Duddy uses high technology to scam his unsuspecting son.

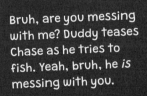

Bruh, are you messing with me? Duddy teases Chase as he tries to fish. Yeah, bruh, he *is* messing with you.

SHE DID IT!

Moomy wins the championship competition of the rice-lift challenge. Boom! Lifted the giant pan filled with rice!

Duddy tries to make strawberry picking more interesting. I'd say he succeeded!

What do Duddy and a mushroom have in common? They're both fun guys! (Ask a biologist if that joke doesn't make sense!)

67

SHAWN BROKE MY TOE!

YouTube sent the FGTeeV family a dope present: a bespoke turntable! With a little setup, the family can play their favorite songs!

First, Duddy must turn the dials to get this antiquated technology working . . .

1:33 AM

Almost there. Just a few more adjustments. Any day now . . .

SOLVING THE MYSTERY OF THE FAKE POWER OUTAGE

Duddy has a swell idea: fake a power outage to teach his family about saving electricity. But can he complete his prank without getting caught?

POWER OUTAGE PRANK — MASTER PLAN

1) SIGN UP FOR FAKE "ELECTRICITY SAVING PROGRAM"

2) SURPRISE!! KILL THE POWER

3) DON'T GET CAUGHT

A foolproof three-step plan! I don't see a problem in the scheme.

Steps one and two go into effect. The family seems to be suspicious. Maybe it's because Duddy is always pulling pranks.

Daddy, did you just mess with something?

DINOSAUR MAZE RACE

To celebrate FGTeeV's book *FGTeeV: Out of Time!*, the family pulls from the pages of their graphic novel and competes in Maze Out of Time! Chase and Moomy team up against Duddz, Mike, and Shawn in the ultimate Cretaceous crackdown.

MIKE FUNNEL DAD FUNNEL MOM CHASE SHAWN

The crew assembles for their rumble in the jungle!

JIM DINOSAUR

TIM ALSO DINOSAUR

Jim (dinosaur) and Tim (also dinosaur) explain how the game works. Basically, remote control your dinosaur. The first team to cross the finish line wins!

Duddy has entered the competition space to sabotage his opponents! I'm not sure that move is in the rule book!

Chase and Moomy operate around Dead Man's Curve.

Duddy and his crew win the top prize, but Moomy might have stolen the golden first-place box! Where could it be?

OREO MOZZARELLA STICKS!

Chef Duddz and Sous-Chef Mike are in the kitchen to cook up some crunchy and cheesy culinary creations. That's right—it's designer mozzarella sticks!

DESIGNER MOZZARELLA STICKS

SPLAT

First up is the fried cheese-puff mozzarella crunch! Chee-sy! Take cheese, flour, eggs, and cheese puffs, and combine and fry to get that golden, delicious crunch!

The next crazy recipe is . . . Wait. The family just wants Duddy to sit down for dinner.

Naw! Instead, it's time for Funyuns, Fritos, Cheetos, and the pièce de résistance: Oreos. Cover your mozzarella sticks in the best snacks to create new Frankenstein creations.

Lexi, the esteemed food critic, gives her Michelin—starred review: they all taste the same. Voilà! Bon appétit!

SPIRIT HALLOWEEN SHOPPING AND UNIVERSAL STUDIOS HORROR NIGHTS

With Halloween right around the corner and Halloween Horror Nights at Universal Studios just over the horizon, it's time for the FGTeeV family to get the right spooky threads to complete their Halloween outfits. Off to the store!

Unspookably scary!

Chase was electrified in the hallway of terror!

THIEVES BROKE INTO OUR HAWAII HOTEL ROOM!

An ideal vacation in the Aloha State (that's Hawaii, by the way) turns into a full-blown investigation into crimes and misdemeanors.

After a tour of Pearl Harbor and the food hall, the family returns to their hotel to find some things have gone missing . . . Like, thirty thousand dollars' worth of stuff! The iPads? Gone. The makeup? Snatched. The family has been robbed!

It's time to call the cops! Gotta get detectives on the case to search for clues. Check the cameras!

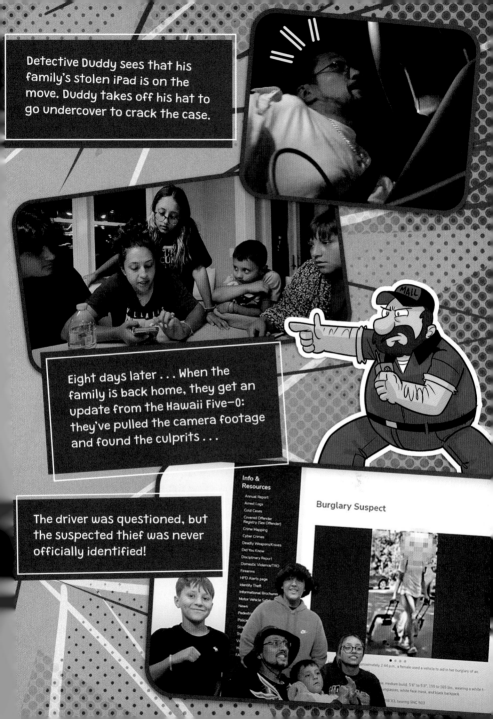

Detective Duddy sees that his family's stolen iPad is on the move. Duddy takes off his hat to go undercover to crack the case.

Eight days later . . . When the family is back home, they get an update from the Hawaii Five-0: they've pulled the camera footage and found the culprits . . .

The driver was questioned, but the suspected thief was never officially identified!

Burglary Suspect

Fine Arts

The **FGTeeV FAMILY** has the **DOPEST SONGS** and the **HIPPEST BEATS.**

"GRANNY'S HOUSE"

Granny is an INSANE survival-horror game. You're locked in Granny's creepy house, and the last thing you want to do is find her!

Dad, do I have to go?
Yes, it'll be fine
Mom?
It's okay sweetie, Granny's awesome
You're gonna have a good time
I don't want to be here

Granny's house, I don't wanna stay
I just wanna go home, I don't wanna be at
Granny's house, she be creeping me out
Take me home right now
I don't wanna stay at
Granny's house, I don't wanna stay
I just wanna go home, I don't wanna be at
Granny's house, she be creeping me out
Take me home right now
I don't wanna stay here

LET'S TAKE A TOUR of the BEST MUSIC VIDEOS of yesterday and today!

Oh jeez, this place gives me the creeps
Hey Granny, I'm here!
Just a minute dear
Is there anything to eat?
Oh, what smells like pickled feet?
Do you wanna play hide-and-seek?

Uh, no thank you, but is your
   TV broke?
And why is the front door so
   locked up so much?
Is that some kinda joke?
Wait, why do you have a bat?
What are you gonna do with that?
Get back! Ow, I think that something cracked

And then I woke up in a different room
Sweating and confused
Did she hit me? 'Cause I'm feeling it
   and I bet she left a bruise
Oh this lady crazy, I've gotta escape
But now there's bear traps that's
   surrounding the place

What am I gonna do? I gotta run
'Cause she's after me but I don't know
   what I've done

(continued...)

Cell phone's only got one bar
Let me try hide and call my mom

Granny's house, something's really weird
I'm feeling kinda scared, please get me
   out of here
Granny's house
She locked all the doors, I can't find the keys
Don't wanna be here no more
Granny's house, I don't wanna stay
I just wanna go home, I don't wanna be at
Granny's house, it's really creeping me out
Take me home right now
I don't wanna stay here

Hello, hello, oh no
Hehe, where'd you go?
Wait, what's that shiny glow?
It's a key! That's what it be!
But what door's it for, I gotta see!
Yes, it's the front door, but there's still a board
I gotta cut a cord and there's another lock?

Now I'm hearing creaks all up the floor
That's coming towards, she's above top
Ran down to the second basement, my face was in shock
'Cause I found a car, but it wouldn't start
Then I got a hammer from the glove box
I see you
Yeah, I'm sure that you do

Now why on Earth in the toilet are there pliers?
I could probably use these to cut the blue wires
Now all I need is the key to escape Granny's house
   so I can be free
Then I got a yellow key, that got me a crossbow
   and tranquilizer (tranquilizer)

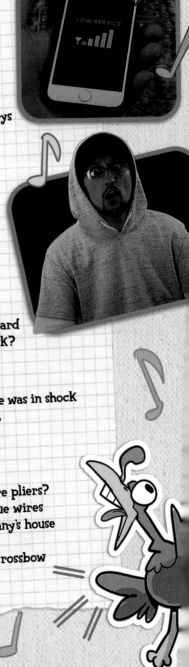

Popped up right behind her,
   then I surprised her
Fired a shot-shot, then she dropped-dropped

Granny's house, now I got the Key
So I'm about to peace out, yeah, it's time
   to leave Granny's house
Time to say goodbye, I feel like I
   could cry, can't believe that I survived
Granny's house, finally getting out
And I'm not looking back, no longer
   trapped at Granny's house
But still I'm all alone, I gotta get home
   but don't Know which way to go

Right now I'm looking for a savior,
   so I went to her neighbor's
"Hello? You gotta help me!"
"Oh yeah! Quick! Get inside!"

"I'M A GURKEY TURKEY"

Sometimes those jump scares make your wobbly knees all gurkey turkey!

Hey-yo pops, wanna play this game?
Nah thanks Kid, that looks lame
No I promise, it's really cool!
Yeah right, it looks old school

No! Try it, you might like it!
All right, don't get so excited
Answer the question
This looks easy
Wait for the next one
The graphics are cheesy

(continued...)

Wait I can't read, what's so funny?
Oh nothing, but you need
    to start running (what?)
He's coming!
Who's coming? What do you mean?
Dad, meet Baldi

Granny hit you with a bat (that's Gurkey)
Neighbor hit you with a trap (that's Gurkey)
Baldi hit you if you're math ain't workin'
When you hear that clap run fast like a turkey

I'm a Gurkey Turkey
Gurkey Turkey, Gurkey Turkey
I'm a Gurkey Turkey
Gurkey Turkey, Gurkey Turkey

So, you wanna try another one?
Yeah, that was kinda fun!
What's up next?
Your pants look wet
Whoops, yep I'll be back real quick

All right, what we gonna play gamer?
It's a game called "Hello Neighbor"
Walk in his house, get to the basement
But watch out, the grouch is waiting

I just gotta open a door, and be sneaky?
I see a key-card, jeez how easy
Oh wait, what, oh, uh, I'm stuck
Is this glue? Ooh-ahh, who's that nut?

What? Hello neighbor
Hey! I mean ahh!
Why in the halls are all these bear traps?
I'm gonna call my mom or my dad
I'm scared again and my pants are all wet

Hmm, maybe we should take a break
No thanks, I'm great okay
I'm not mistaken, I know I can make it
See I did it!
Get out of my basement

Granny hit you with a bat (that's Gurkey)
Neighbor hit you with a trap (that's Gurkey)
Baldi hit you if you're math
    ain't workin'
When you hear that clap run
    fast like a turkey

I'm a Gurkey Turkey
Gurkey Turkey, Gurkey Turkey
I'm a Gurkey Turkey
Gurkey Turkey, Gurkey Turkey

This next one might get ya messy
Why?
'Cause we're playin' bendy
Oh! So what's that mean?
I forgot to tell you 'bout the ink
    machine!
It's spawning faulty creatures and
    a heap of ink
That seeks to keep from being extinct

Whoa, whoa, whoa, whoa, whoa
What the poop, is that bacon soup?
Are you listening?
Yeah without a doubt, it's like Mickey Mouse
Whoa, it's getting dark, what's this about?
How do I get out? What's that sound? Ow!
I've got you now

Boris cut in half (that's Gurkey)
Freddy jump you in FNAF (that's Gurkey)
Slendrina, I don't mean to be mean or nuthin'
But I'm not lovin' your face, it's Gurkey

I'm a Gurkey Turkey
Gurkey Turkey, Gurkey Turkey
I'm a Gurkey Turkey
Gurkey Turkey, Gurkey Turkey
(Gurkey, Gurkey Turkey)

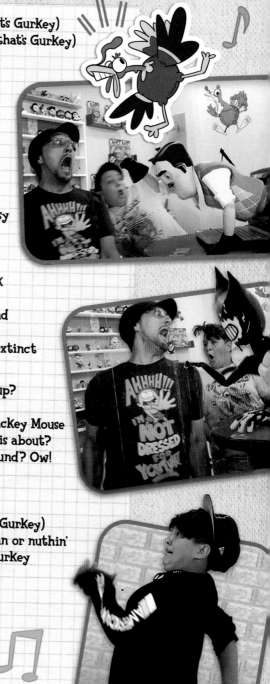

"PSYCHO PIG"

"Psycho Pig" is the Bloxy Award—winning song and music video about the psycho pig that's coming for Duddy!

I got a story 'bout a psycho pig
She's coming for me, she's a psycho pig, she's crazy
I don't know what I did to psycho pig
Running for my life from a psycho pig

Yo, whose house is this, house is this?
Don't know, but I gotta get out of it
(Where am I?)
All the doors have been locked up
I'mma find a nice little spot on the
 couch to sit

Yo, danger is definite
Why is there so many pictures of
 Peppa Pig?
What in the heck is this?
I'm getting really freaked out
That's when I see her just creepin' about

WHAT IN THE HECK IS THIS?

I'm moving as fast as I can
Be all on my back with a bat like she Granny
Hid in the kitchen, she finds me I'm through
Oh, there's some pizza, don't mind if i do
This weirdo's near, this gear goes here
I'm burning the rubber on my Nikes
Broke two by fours on the door
Put the code in then busted out with
 the white key

Think I was kidnapped by a psycho pig
She really did that, she's a psycho pig,
  she's crazy!
I don't know what I did to psycho pig
Running for my life from a psycho pig

Went up in the school on the very next day
I was up in class, I'm writing an essay
Heard the bell ring, and I jumped out my seat
But the boarded up door was there blocking the way

Yo, she must've followed me here
The end is probably near
She got the creepiest eye, and I see the evil inside
But she got the floppiest ears (aww)

But that isn't Piglet, no this one is different
And she's on a mission to find me
I found me a book, and I put it in place
But yo, I wasn't looking behind me
I picked up the carrot and gave it to bunny
  while running
And she took the heat for me to pick up the key
Run to the door, bust the lock open
  with it and leave

I'm so exhausted from this psycho pig
She's really lost it, she's a psycho pig, she's crazy
I don't know what I did to psycho pig
Running for my life from a psycho pig

It's chapter ten, see
Pull up to the mall on my 10-speed
I lent my brotha the Bentley
Kick down the stand, and then
  watch 'em all flip
While I'm making my entry
Then she... (what?) came outta Kohl's
  with a mean mug
Poured out my cup and said "Clean up"
Listen here piggy, but you and you
  homies existing offends me

(continued...)

Then she grabbed on to my collar and
    gave me a wedgie
And took about twenty-two dollars,
    called me a doody head
Truly, man, she made me cry until
    I went and called for my momma
I don't know why she's so mean
    to me
I was just trying to get me some pizza
See, I wish it wasn't, it is
But I admit, I got beat up by a psycho pig

Man, I got beat up by this psycho pig
Got no idea why this psycho pig's so angry
She really whooped me, she's a psycho pig
Running for my life from a psycho pig

Psycho pig, psycho pig, psycho
Psycho pig (psycho)
Psycho pig, psycho pig, psycho
Psycho pig (psycho)
Like a psycho pig, psycho pig, psycho
Psycho pig (psycho)
Like a psycho pig,
    psycho pig, psycho
Psycho pig (psycho)

I got a
story 'bout
a psycho pig
She's coming for me,
she's a psycho pig,
she's crazy
I don't know what I
did to psycho pig
Running for my life
from a psycho
pig, oh no

I GOT BEAT UP BY A PSYCHO PIG

"ANT BULLY"

Going to school, having a job, or being a good family member is hard work. It's tough to be an ant climbing that hill every day, but it's even tougher when there's an ant bully who walks all over you.

I SMASH!!

Duddy knows what it's like to have an ant bully make your life more difficult.

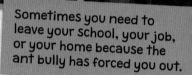

The ant bully pounds the mound the ants were constructing.

Sometimes you need to leave your school, your job, or your home because the ant bully has forced you out.

YOU A BULLY

But the bigger the ant bully, the harder they fall.

With the whole team behind you, you can take down real-life bullies.

"THE OTHER SIDE (GREENER GRASS)"

Sometimes jealousy or longing can take control of our thoughts, but we should always count the blessings we already have.

CHECK OUT THE CHORUS

They say the grass is greener on the other side
But that's a lie.

There's one thing that you gotta know
Everybody has a story to be told.

I'm certain that everybody hurting behind their curtain.

There can't be flowers without rain.

So always, live your life, don't let it fly by.

"SLAY ALL DAY"

Stay humble but enjoy your success! Slay all day!

CHECK OUT THE CHORUS

It's about to snow

Makin' a difference
while makin' a livin'

Know it's quality over
quantity all the way

Done with all the wannabes

We play harder
(Slay all,
slay all day)

"WALK LIKE SHAWN"

Baby Shawn started a new dance craze. Duddy shows Mike and Lexi all the steps so they can walk like Shawn. You can too!

HOW TO DO THE SHAWN!

ZOMBIE-ARMS

Step one:
Pop your belly out!

Step two:
Put your zombie arms up!

Step three:
Put a bowl between your legs!

Now put it all together! Belly out, zombie arms, bow legs, and now walk like Shawn!

"I WANT SOME McDONALD'S"

The FGTeeV family decides to make a quick dash to McDonald's to scarf down some chicken nuggies. I hope everything goes okay . . .

CHECK OUT THE CHORUS

I just wanted McDonald's
So I went to McDonald's
But I swear this dude Ronald,
   he really got it out for me
(And I'm just trying to eat)
I just wanted McDonald's
So I went to McDonald's
But I swear this dude Ronald,
   he really got it out for me

YAY!

HE REALLY GOT IT OUT FOR ME

NOOBS ONLY RESTROOM

NOOBS ONLY RESTROOM

"APE CHASE"

FGTeeV's *Ape Chase* is the fun platformer by the FGTeeV crew. Play as all your favorite characters!

Here comes that ape!

Duddy's gotta dodge those ape attacks!

Every character is raring to go! You've got your cop, your Revolutionary War general, your Wild West prospector. All the fan favorites!

Kablammo!

Spooked that ape!

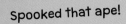

"BAD BREATH (FNAF STYLE)"

When you're stuck at Freddy's for five nights, you're gonna find yourself the center of attention. Even so, you must decline. You need to brush your teeth because you've got some bad breath!

THINGS DUDDY'S BREATH SMELLS LIKE:

—Deviled eggs
—Garbage stuffed into fish
—Steamed vegetables
—Gym socks on a crusty, musty clown
—Moldy chicken
—Fungus on a sponge
—Pickled kitty litter
—Donkey dung

"PARTY IN THE ELEVATOR"

In classic FGTeeV tradition, any elevator can become a dance hall, and suddenly you have a party as you're going up the floors. Come along as they get their rock on!

These club goers are looking for the perfect dance party.

WE DONT NEED A CLUB?

PARTY, PARTY

Lexi and Mike get down to that sick beat!

Skip McGiggleson is DJing this off-the-hook kickback. I know him! He's my friend!

PAR

Raise the roof! Literally!

WHO WANNA PARTY, PARTY, PARTY, IN THE ELEVATOR

Lexi knows how to boogie!

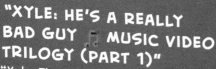

"XYLE: HE'S A REALLY BAD GUY　MUSIC VIDEO TRILOGY (PART 1)"

"Xyle: The Music Video Trilogy" is the villain origin story of Kyle, A.K.A. Xyle, the sore loser of FeeGee's youth.

In the glory days of video-game arcades, FeeGee (the once and future Duddy) was the best gamer in the arcade hall.

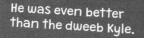

He was even better than the dweeb Kyle.

But Kyle transformed into his villainous alter ego, Xyle! He got muscles and everything.

And Xyle followed through on his evil plot to take control of every video game ever made!

Sometimes, if you can't be the hero, you become the bad guy!

To be continued . . .

"XYLE: CUTTING THE CONSOLE MUSIC VIDEO TRILOGY (PART 2)"

In the exciting continuation of the Xyle saga, FeeGee uses time travel to battle Xyle and play the villain at his own games.

While all the best games have been consumed by Xyle, FeeGee has an idea.

The boys go back to the past to fix the future!

In a montage of history's best games, Duddy must brawl Xyle in each one!

Duddy won't let Xyle get away with what he's done!

Xyle explains he became evil when FeeGee humiliated him, but Xyle's memory isn't quite right . . .

To be continued . . .

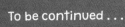

98

"XYLE: CLOSING THE MULTIVERSE 🎵 MUSIC VIDEO TRILOGY (PART 3)"

In the thrilling conclusion of the Xyle saga, Duddy must fix the tears in the multiverse!

Classic game characters come up with plans A and B. Plan A: ask Xyle to close the rips in the multiverse. Plan B: punch Xyle.

With the power of the mightiest video-game characters, Duddy is ready to finish this fight.

But Xyle fights back with everything he's got!

Still, Duddy takes down Xyle, and the portals close one by one.

Xyle is finally banished through the last portal to Galaga, where he vows to get revenge one day.

Sports

THIS YEAR'S GRADUATING CLASS HAS BEEN OUR GREATEST CROP OF E-SPORTSMEN.

From acting all sus in *Among Us* to platforming to their doom in *Roblox*, from escaping Theodore Peterson in *Hello Neighbor* to collecting the perfect resources in *Minecraft*, our **FGTeeV** e–athletes **RACK UP THE HIGH SCORES** and **PUT THE HURT** on all their rivals.

GRANNY

Granny is an indie survival-horror video game. In the game, you must use your wits to outsmart Granny's puzzles and traps to escape the house.

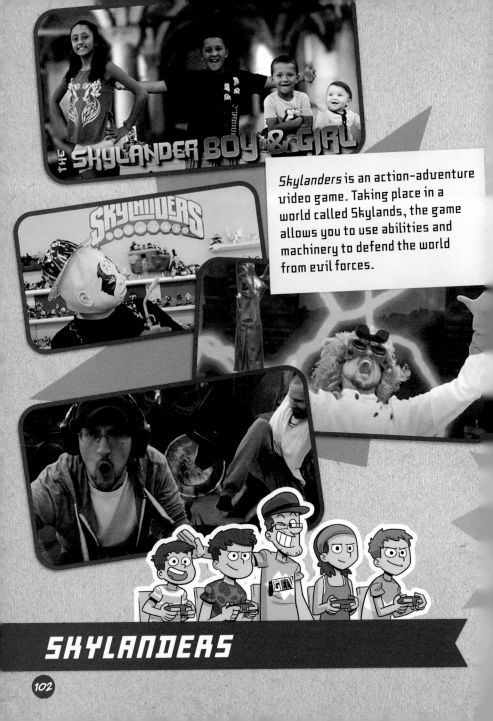

Skylanders is an action-adventure video game. Taking place in a world called Skylands, the game allows you to use abilities and machinery to defend the world from evil forces.

SKYLANDERS

The Baby in Yellow is a creepy horror game. You take on the role of a babysitter who must take care of a sinister baby.

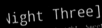

Night Three]
Sitter: "Good night. Sweet dreams."
The Child: "I will show you my dreams."

Press Here To Start

PPA TAPPA

TAPPA

Talking Ben the Dog is a simulation game. You talk to a grumpy dog named Ben and try to get him to respond to you.

TALKING BEN THE DOG

POPPY PLAYTIME

Poppy Playtime is a horror puzzle game. You take the role of a former employee of a toy-making company who discovers the staff has disappeared for sinister reasons.

Hello Neighbor is a survival-horror stealth game where you must learn and solve the secrets of your crazy neighbor by exploring his spooky house. The FGTeeV family loves to play all the games in the *Hello Neighbor* universe and often finds themselves surprised by jump scares.

HELLO NEIGHBOR

GANG BEASTS

DUDDY

LEXI

MIKE

MOOMY

SHAWN

CHASE

Gang Beasts is a beat 'em up party game where players toss their friends from billboards and body slam them in the wrestling ring.

Loading
Menu

ROBLOX

Roblox is an online game creation and social platform where gamers can play and make games. The FGTeeV family loves to play all the games on the platform, like *Prop Hunt X Hide and Seek*, *Doors*, and *Rainbow Friends*.

FLOPPY MINECRAFT

The most successful game of all time, *Minecraft* is a sandbox game where players use their blocky characters to build, fight, gather, and explore! FGTeeV loves the crafting abilities in *Minecraft*.

RESPAWN

MINECRAFT

AMONG US

Among Us is the online multiplayer social deduction game where you play as a crewmate (or an imposter) and try to secure victory for your team. The entire FGTeeV crew heads down to the movie theater to play Among Us on the big screen! Game on!

Five Nights at Freddy's is a point-and-click survival-horror game. You're stuck in a pizzeria with a bunch of animatronic characters, and if you don't defend yourself, those homicidal mechanoids will get you!

FIVE NIGHTS AT FREDDY'S

BENDY AND THE INK MACHINE

Bendy and the Ink Machine is a spooky first-person survival-horror video game where you must navigate your old animation studio and avoid Bendy at all costs!

INK

Sometimes the floor turns to lava and there ain't nothing you can do about it! In the game *The Floor Is Lava* you need to make sure you stay on the furniture and not dip your toes into the lava.

THE FLOOR IS LAVA

FINDING BIGFOOT

Crikey! There's a bigfoot on the loose, and Duddy and Chase are just the blokes to find him. They'll have to sneak through the jungle in the *Finding Bigfoot* game and hope they don't get eaten by the beast himself!

Baldi, from *Baldi's Basics in Education and Learning*, loves to give out quarters for correct answers. But he loves partying in the elevator even more!

BALDI'S BASICS

Choo-Choo Charles is an indie horror game where players upgrade their train's defenses to fend off the creepy Charles, a spider-train hybrid monster.

Derailed.

Where Are They Now?

KING CRAB

Fell into a hot pot of creamy soup and became chowder.

EVIL ZEEBUB

Inadvertently shrunk himself in his evil lair and is still trying to climb up to hit the reverse button on the Creatasize 500 machine.

POSTAL JENKINS

Finally retired and is now at home driving Mrs. Jenkins crazy.

RAPTAIN HOOK & SQUAWX

Went on a treasure hunt and is lost at sea but surely listening to some cool beats.

We've said goodbye to so many **WONDERFUL CHARACTERS** over the years, so let's check in with our **ESTEEMED ALUMNI** to find out what they've been up to out in that **WILD WORLD**!

CLARENCE

Is now running a Fortune 500 company that sells insurance with his cousin the Gecko.

DUCAS WINSTON

Decided to enroll at Plushie Academy to get his master's degree in squish. He has a whole lot of homework to do, but Ducas Winston is the kind of guy who buckles down and studies.

SKINNY BONZ

Joined the gym, bulked up, and started entering body-building competitions. Now he no longer goes by Skinny Bonz and instead goes by Swole Bonz.

DARLA

Darla the goat, best known for crashing the FGTeeV family pad, has been studying abroad for the past year. She's not exactly sure what she's studying or where she's studying, but she's making the most of it.

Into the World!

OUR WARMEST **CONGRATULATIONS** to this year's graduating class of **LOVABLE SCAMPS!**

COME BACK AND VISIT!

Lovable Scamps

Glossary

BRUH: an expression of bro love, bro frustration, or gamer rage

CALLIE: sweet baby sister puppy . . . with a secret rambunctious side

CHASE: A.K.A. LightCore Chase, FGTeeV Chase, Drizz McNizz, Drizzy, Chase-Tsu, King of Roblox

CRINGE: super embarrassing or awkward

DUDDY: A.K.A. Duddz, FeeGee, Skylander Dad, FUNnel Dad, and BEST DAD EVER

FGTeeV: Family Gaming Teams' Extraordinarily Entertaining Videos

FUNnel Boy: The totally iconic mascot of FUNnel Vision and FGTeeV. His real name is Skip McGiggleson.

GLIZZY: hot dog

LEXI: A.K.A. Lex, FGTeeV Lex, Skylander Girl, and (of course) @lex_0724 on TikTok

MIKE: A.K.A. Michael, Skylander Boy, and the best dancer who has ever lived

MOOMY: A.K.A. Not—So—Skylander Mom and FUNnel Mom. Don't call her Mommy!

NOOB: a newbie with zero gamer skillz

OLLIE: Snuggle buddy extraordinaire

OREO: the OG cutie—pie Christmas present puppy dog!

ROASTED: Total disrespect. If someone gives you a sick burn, you're *so* roasted!

SHAWN: A.K.A. FGTeeV Shawn, Beasty, Ghost Puncher, Skybaby (back in the day!)

SLAY: No, this doesn't mean to slay your enemies in *Fortnite*. It means to be AWESOME!

SUS: Suspicious. Like Moomy venting in *Among Us*!

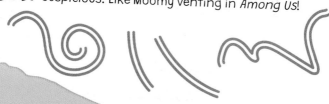

The Yearbook Committee

EDITOR-IN-CHIEF
FUNnel Boy
(A.K.A. SKIP McGIGGLESON)

ADVISERS
DERPY BACON
& mEGGz

MANAGING EDITOR
POSTAL JENKINS

LAYOUT EDITOR
GURKEY TURKEY

DESIGNER
BAGGO BEANS

COPY EDITOR
FRANKLIN GARFUNKEL
TeeV

WRITER
BLOBBYFISH

PHOTO EDITOR
NEIL

PHOTOGRAPHER
GAMER BRAT

REGULAR REPORTER
MILO

ADVERTISING MANAGER
BIG BABY

PUBLISHER
COLONEL CORN

LEAD REPORTER
GOATY

LEAD REPORTER
WOODROW

INDEX EDITOR
CHEF DUDDY

Xyle

mask off (e

EMPEROR
(CECIL)

FGTEEV

Lieutenant
Lambchop

Sergeant
Sirloin

Autographs

Have your best friends sign your copy of FGTeeV: The Official Guidebook!

FGTeeV
DUddy

Moomy

Chase